The One Who Swears
You Can't Start Over

ETHNA McKIERNAN

for Hillary,

from one of her biggest

Laurel Hell fans!

Affectionately,

Ethna McKiernan

salmonpoetry

Published in 2002 by
Salmon Publishing Ltd,
Cliffs of Moher, Co. Clare, Ireland
www.salmonpoetry.com
email: info@salmonpoetry.com

A catalogue record for this book is available from the British Library.

The Arts Council   Salmon Publishing gratefully acknowledges the
An Chomhairle Ealaíon financial assistance of the Arts Council.

ISBN 1 903392 22 5

Cover photography: Jessie Lendennie
Cover design & typesetting: Siobhán Hutson
Printed by Offset Paperback Mfrs. Inc., PA

For Naoise, Conor and Brian

Acknowledgements

Some of these poems have appeared in the following anthologies and journals:

33 Minnesota Poets (Minneapolis, MN), *An Céidhe* (Ireland), *Books Ireland* (Dublin) *Eclectic Literary Forum* (Tonawanda, NY), *Here's Me Bus!* (New York, NY), *Minnesota Monthly* (St. Paul, MN), *The Minnesota Poetry Calendar* (Goodhue, MN), *The Next Parish Over* (New Rivers Press, Minneapolis, MN), *New Hibernia Review* (St. Paul, MN), *The North Coast Review* (Duluth, MN), *The North Stone Review* (Minneapolis, MN), *Poetry Ireland Review* (Dublin), *The Santa Barbara Independent* (Santa Barbara, CA), *Sidewalks* (Anoka, MN), *The Squaw Valley Review* (Squaw Valley, CA) and *The White Page/An Bhileog Bhán: Twentieth Century Irish Women Poets* (Salmon Publishing, Co. Clare, Ireland).

Thanks to my writing community at home, on the east and west coasts, and the other side of the Atlantic.

Contents

III – The Poverty of Secrets

IV – Of Boys And Men

V – The One Who Swears You Can't Start Over

Later

When you press the oars
into the river, the boat moves
forward. You're surprised
a moment – B follows A after all,
and the world goes on.

It's like this, these days –
the muscle building slowly
in your arms as you navigate
the green boat alone,
your lungs stretching further

with each oar-stroke.
You row toward the deep waters,
humming the first bars
of that song you'd thought
had drowned.

What The Light Leaves

Barn Burning

The barn burned all night,
its black ribs alive and bare
against the orange glow.
How I wanted to enter
its great light, to slip on
the exquisite dress sewn
from tips of flame, test
the weightless shoes of white ash
waiting there for me
since birth.
When the hulk of roof
finally fell in hot chunks
at my feet, I would pocket
two small pieces of its history
and walk unscathed
out to the long wet grasses
just beyond the barn,
where I would press my body
to the green earth
until it seared an imprint
there. And then I would
memorize
again and yet again
the outline of the lit barn
and its lean bones;
the world charged suddenly
as baptism, my life changed
forever with the knowledge
of fire.

The Otherworld

Only ninety steps from house to forest.
I counted them, summer days, my whole body
pulled like a magnet toward the green light
humming through the thick stand of pines.
It was the otherworld I craved, the air
silver with dust-motes floating down between
deep green needles, the pitch of pine-scent
tuned tightly to a high thin note,
the forest floor worn and soft as an old rug,
and all the lure of foreign places calling.

We danced there, my sisters and I,
twirling our gypsy skirts for an audience
of mute trees in the clearing. By noon
we were heady with possibility
of claiming the lost Irish crown, the coveted role
of Queen Kathleen, Ruler of the Forest.

And each day ended with my mother's voice
sounding the dinner-call, pulling us back
again. While we ate, while
we played, every hour surged forward
and away from us into the future,
and never once as we filled our lungs
with great gulps of sweet green air
did we consider this.

Dress-Ups

I was the gypsy with the mismatched scarves,
torn petticoats and practiced foreign air.
Nuala was the princess, her blue-black hair
like night on snow, regal curls tumbling down
around the cape my mother had fashioned
from the white lace slip she hadn't worn
since the ninth child's birth.

A coven of giggly girls we were, deep
in the land of dress-ups, pure babes
at the altar of artifice, the sweet
imaginary world of grown-up women
sensed through fingertips as we stroked pink
organza, cinched the faded blue satin blouse
around our waists with old rope, dreamed
of marriages we wouldn't yet know for years,

of silky nights of August heat
with our discarded costumes flung
across some chair, skins bare at last
of any fabric but the soft chenille coverlet
resting on our legs.

Those Girls

They never learn, those girls.
At seven, shut out from the clubhouse,
they simply wait it out.
Come fourteen, each one
will allow some boy
the buttons to her blouse, believing
certainly, he loves her now.
They fall hard, marry early
and at thirty wonder
where the years went,
why their longing lingers still.

Women now, they spend their thirst
on men who cannot quench it,
cowboys with deserts in their hearts.
The sun sets and rises; sets again
to men who daily break these women open
with unfaithfulness, a nod, a fist,
a word, the silence of refusal
or a simple walk away.

Those girls, they'll never learn,
their eyes mesmerized and glittering
with moon. I watch their moth-like arms
reaching outward to the fire, watch
them singe and burn with pain
every time they stretch those arms
toward that reckless red flame
some call love.

DUFOUR EDITIONS

Thank you for purchasing this book. For a free catalogue of our other titles that are available from better booksellers, please complete and return this card.

Name: _____

Address: _____

City: _____ State: _____ Zip: _____

Please indicate your areas of special interest:

- [ ] Children's Books
- [ ] Dance, Drama, Theatre
- [ ] History
- [ ] Irish Studies
- [ ] Slavic Studies
- [ ] Gay & Lesbian
- [ ] Literary Criticism
- [ ] Germanic Studies
- [ ] Poetry
- [ ] Religion & Philosophy

- [ ] Scottish Studies
- [ ] Mystery / Crime Fiction
- [ ] Welsh Studies
- [ ] Women's Studies
- [ ] Scandinavian Studies
- [ ] Crafts, Hobbies, Cooking
- [ ] Folklore
- [ ] Other _____
- [ ] Other _____
- [ ] Other _____

1-800-869-5677 • www.dufoureditions.com • info@dufoureditions.com • Fax: 610-458-7103

Dufour Editions
P.O. Box 7
Chester Springs, PA 19425-0007

Mountain / The Longing

Without force, explosives
or even a hand-held drill,
I wanted to enter
the mountain tonight.
I wanted to enter quietly,
the way a man at peace
enters the woman he loves
and lives with his longing
to swim up her wet skin
to the secret heart
of her, wrapping
that knowledge around him
forever.

    Call it desire
without lust or urgency,
an ancient beckoning
to touch the core
behind the shell, to stroke
the smooth inner bulk of granite,
float in rock and earth
like one of its pores or cells
until the mountain and I
became one thing
undivided by form.

    I wanted
to enter the mountain tonight
to hear the wind rushing
through some crevice there,
a voice I've craved all my life
calling, calling me home.

Beginning To Name It: Poetry

It is the strange vegetable
that grows outside the garden,
at once pocked and luminous.
It is the one nutrient
your body longs for
when you feel nothing
but hunger and desire,
bent double with the need
for even a morsel of its blue leaves.
It is the mystery scientists
spend late-night hours researching
and the speech of wind in an empty room;
it falls from the sleeping child's mouth
in a whimper or a sigh, it lies
quietly in file cabinets, the small ink
alphabets pulsing straight through metal.
And at any moment in this world
it can seize you with its reckless song
or water the desert hidden
in your heart. Shyly, it may ask you
for the next dance alone
and at evening's end, brand you
with the fire of its necessary name.

Why I Lied My Way Through Childhood

Because I loved the textured detail
fiction added to the ordinary real,
the dull navy Easter coat embroidered
with elaborate gold brocade instead.
Because I'd read *Pippi Longstocking*
so many times I couldn't help believe
she truly was my cousin and we'd lived
together every summer on that island.
Because the landscape of fact was plain
as fishstick-Fridays in Lent, and what harm
was there imagining I'd turned the dial
on Mrs. Hewitt's birth-control pills
a few notches forward when babysitting,
bragging to disbelieving friends
there'd be another baby in the year?
Because I *liked* the sympathy the nuns
doled like warm honey when they learned
I had leukemia at sixteen.
Because it's well-known the Irish are prone
to hyperbole, and because my parents
refused me acting lessons, holding out
for violin. Because I always wanted
the world to be bigger than it is.
Telling my children tonight about the time
I won Merlin's sword in a stone-toss,
I know they know this is the utter truth
from Mom's childhood.

The Poet Finds New Formulae

*after a remark by a well-known poet about his new working ritual of
writing a poem a day in bed before arising, enjoying his coffee as he writes*

In my retirement, I, too, vow to write
a poem a day before leaving bed.
There will be coffee first, of course, heaped
with cream and served by a young man
eager to please. Three gulps I need before
the words can even start homing in
toward the poem... Then I'll stretch and drink
and consider the placement of commas,
debate with myself about whether the epic
or the lyric is best-suited for the day.
When the poem's done and all the coffee
gone, the young man will draw my bath
and I will arise bursting with virtue,
humming with caffeine, grateful
for the training my young man received
before landing his internship
with this older poet sailing in her prime.

How tiresome it gets amidst these covers
in the afternoon sun! Long past noon
and I'm still drumming an arthritic finger
on blank paper, pleading with recalcitrant
words which will not line up with the others,
pounding stubborn images into bloom. Fury
builds in me as I cancel one appointment,
then the next. When the boy asks discreetly
whether Madam wishes for an afternoon snack,
something snaps and I yank his hair,
then call the agency, demanding
a replacement. Oh, to write one sestina
by the time night falls – to toss the stale coffee
down the drain, peel back the years
and start again!

Snow White Revived

"Mirror, mirror on the wall"
was how the whole thing started,
my stepmother trembling at the threshold
of middle age, her radiant beauty
just about to fade. Innocent
of the mirror's lure, I wore my black hair
in braids, knew each tree
in the forest by its bark, conversed
with thrush and lark as I played.

So you can see that when the prince
plucked the poisonous apple
from between my lips,
I couldn't bear the joy in his eyes.
What lay ahead was someone else's destiny,
tiresome curtseys and the weight of a crown;
a closet full of wasp-waisted dresses
and villagers "your highnessing" me
right and left, with all the expectations
of a man who'd saved my life
waiting for me in bed at night.

All I'd really wanted was to dwell
in harmony among the dwarves,
playing Scrabble at the breakfast table
with the little men I loved, Doc and Sleepy
waving as they walked out the door
to the mines, Bashful and Dopey
singing a duet while we washed the morning dishes.

But the drama's fizzled into history
long ago – the huntsman who spared my neck,
the trick of combs and apples, the fact

of my survival. God knows why,
but one morning I unbound my braids
and stepped into the palace for the first time.
My hair slid down my shoulders
and I shivered as it settled
on the weight of red brocade below.

How I miss playing house
with that band of doting dwarves,
how I can't explain to Hans
I preferred the apple in my throat
to this queenship I pretend is mine.

Peter Flees Galilee For The Mountains

Can I tell you what the journey has been like?
My sandals nearly ground to dust,
my legs heavy as stone pillars
at day's end, the robust sea-air
leaving my lungs which fill instead
with the thin broth of high altitude.

Everything was simple before
he said my name: *Peter*, like that,
and suddenly my life of nets
and fish diminished into gestures
of no consequence.
The broad sea lost its lustre,
the sun flattened out the hills
and I was his.

Now I have been travelling for weeks
to escape his face, that voice
an arrow shooting toward my boat,
my shuttered heart, homing in
on every hidden cell.

I thought that once out of my element
I'd forget, the bulk and height of land
above my head so foreign
it would obliterate the past
with its sheer mass, its power.

But when I press my skin
against the granite cheeks of the mountain
I hear him deep inside the rock,
calling me again.
Lord, is there nowhere on this earth
that I can hide?

What The Light Leaves

How quickly light slips from the sky
at dusk – the pink yolks of mirrored clouds
in the lake sliding into runny grey,
the elongated water-twin of the aspen
snapping backward to its landbound self.
Above, the heron's broad wing-swoop streaks
and blurs as inch by inch, the natural world
sinks into darkness. This is the kingdom of sound
now, the country of enormous blindness
where crickets congregate in song
and fish arc and splash above the lake
unseen, where the forest cracks and rustles
to its own percussive tune, where every map
is useless and the gravel trail back to the car
disappears. Only the intermittent sparks
of light from my beloved fireflies,
their half-extinct flickerings
hovering like small luminaries
around the outline of my lover's hand, only
the wind-kindled lake lapping the shore
like an echo of sighs into sleep.

Reds

I'm gathering reds to store for my journey –
the ruby jewels of school bus lights,
their bright urgency, their warning;
the heat of red geraniums pulsing
from a wooden pot on a stranger's porch;
a red metal woodpecker, flecks
of chipped paint peeling from his chest
like rusty feathers falling to the ground;
even the red fire hydrant at the corner,
though I know its weight is enormous
for such a trip as this. And because
it is cold in the country where I'm headed,
I will choose the tiny red blaze
of a child's jacket as it bobs along
the breakwall to the harbor; willing him,
as I watch, to surrender one small part
of his red unbroken heart,
and hand it to me as his parting gift.

The Architecture Of Flowers

Inside the drum of petals
yellow-cropped stamens
shake gold dust from anthers.
They are a stand of miniature trees,
tall as thumbnails, wide
as a strand of hair.
If I could pull myself up
their silky ropes, I would leap
into the rouged bowl
of this orange columbine
and wander through the chambers
of its complicated heart
until I reached the room
of childhood, where I would taste
again my father's oatmeal
in the chilly Dublin kitchen
before dawn, breathe
my mother's lily-of-the-valley smell
at bathtime, unknow roses
sheared off by the storm
or the bitter rages
of the father of my children.
From there I would walk down
the long halls and crannies
of flowerdom until I found
the honey-nub of peace,
and in that room
I would freeze, raise
my arms high as irises,
hard as trumpet blasts, urge
the whole future
to stop, now, at once.

Alzheimer's Weather

"A pity beyond all telling
Is hid in the heart of love…"
    W. B. Yeats

Alzheimer's Weather

At first the weather was mild,
scattered showers at most
or the occasional dim hint of lightning.
She'd laugh when she'd forgotten
where she parked the car,
and so would we.

Lately now it seems a kind of static's
playing havoc with her brain
as small gaps of time explode into oblivion,
the way the weight of January snow
snapped the one brittle branch
off the burr oak last year
and suddenly a space blank as loss appeared
among the tangle of black branches.

All my life I've been afraid of thunder,
hiding, once, under my desk at 2:00 a.m.
in the old place on Selby over Captain Ken's.
I don't know why she doesn't reel or jump
the way I do when it booms through the sky,
or whether it's just one more sound
added to the clamor humming there
between her ears.

How I'd like to hold her as the slow tornado
approaches, how we'd all like to save her
from the darkness of the storm.
But her children have become remote

as third cousins, blurred shadows
indistinct as any raindrops
splashed on summer windows.

The burden of memory is to feel pain:
I pray she doesn't own it. Let her mistake
me for her sister and I'll gladly answer
in the present tense; let my father's banter
serve as courtship once again. Let
her small world keep her safe from any harm,
and in the stillness of amnesia
let her never know the sting or fury
of the desert wind.

Theft

Last night I stole her blue beaded necklace,
the one I'd given her some past Christmas.
While she sat in her favorite flowered chair
tracking dust motes under the table lamp,
I slipped the string of beads
into the zipper pocket of my black purse.

When the dead leave, what is left to clutch?
All the rough intangibles become so much dust,
flour sifting downward from a torn bag.
Some raw material thing becomes necessity,
an article which owns the memory of perfume
or holds the far remembered cry of a voice
calling us in summer on the fevered afternoons
we'd stray too deep into the lake.

She won't miss it now, the necklace,
a minor theft when held against this largest loss
of all. I watch her press her hands to her head
asking where in God's name it has disappeared,
who has sacked her life and carried off her very mind,
who the robber, what the theft, when the larceny occurred,
Jesus, why.

Birthday

At 75, she's a small girl again,
singing her own "Happy Birthday"
as we lay the cake before her.
Candles light her eyes the way
they did at ten, when the pretty curls
her mother brushed spun loops around her head.

It's so confusing who the birthday girl
is, so many children mixing up
the present with the past. My thin father
tells her that he loves her,
and she becomes nineteen
in pale blue formal dress, anxious
as she brushes flecks of dirt from white gloves
in the subways of New York
where they will meet in 1935.

Now she walks across the dining room
to a photo of an older sister,
kisses it and turns to us as if
the keeper of a grand secret.
"I like this girl," she says, "because
her family's so polite, because she always
buys me nice clothes."

When everyone has left and hours have passed
since my sisters sanely entered sleep,
she'll pull her bureau scarf and all
her pretty jars roughly to the floor
and she will scream. I've become the demon

That I always was to her,
she'll threaten the police unless
I bring my father back again,
she'll rant and weep and plead for different years,
she'll smash the green Belgian glass
two inches from my head
even as she curses this disease,

a pained, heavy woman
in her 76th year, holding me,
the difficult daughter incapable of tears.

Absences

Cell by cell my mother is leaving us.
No one can stop the memory leaking
from her body in such helpless cupfuls,
the way flecks of dead skin disappear
and scatter into air like loose dust gone wild
when brushed from sun-dried flesh.

The lost language in her eyes,
my face before hers like a question-mark,
her vision blank with Haldol
or bright with terror,
a terrible incomprehension
stuttering through her body –

I hear the doctors say her brain
has atrophied a few degrees
beyond the CT scan of last year,
and I see a border of grey air
circling that unprotected, shrunken mass,
empty spaces wind could rattle through,
small animals could chatter in.

The howl at the door. Each day, every night.
Down the road, a gravesite beckoning.
My body like a fetus, curled in mute rage
on the floor near her bed. Selfish
as an infant, wondering who will know us now,
when we were children.

My mother, in all her Irish beauty,
singing suddenly at 3:00 a.m.:
"The violets were scenting the woods, Maggie,
displaying their charms to the breeze,
when I first said I loved only you, Maggie,
and you said you loved only me."
My father, weeping.

Night Shift

She went down like an angel into sleep
tonight, serene and rosy after dinner,
every struggle of the day a deep
thing shrugged away into the blur
of slumber. Such gifts as this are pure
jewels after nights of strain,
weeks of fending off dementia's gain.

Potatoes

Someone is weeping in the kitchen.
It is my father, crying quietly
as he peels the dinner potatoes.
He pierces their white hearts with a fork
and steam rises upward toward his beard.
Below, hot tears salt the bowl.
The intimacy of the moment staggers,
as when I stumbled, once, as a child,
upon him cupping my mother's face
in broad, noon daylight as they entered
the deep, private zone of a kiss.
How could he have known, when he made
that vow fifty-seven years ago,
how suddenly and readily she'd leave him —
pork chops burnt, potatoes blackening
over gas — for that thin stranger
called Alzheimer, waltzing through
the kitchen door like a suitor
who has never lost a single lover's hand
he's played?

She Enters The Nursing Home

This isn't my mother, the woman in the wheelchair
crooning to the doll who never leaves her arms.
Neither is she among those lined up
in the rows beneath the fish-tank,
all staring blankly upward at the tiny
orange bodies flitting left and right.

It's hard to find her here among so many
who appear alike. When I spot her
by the window in the hallway, she is rocking
back and forth against her chair strap,
fist raised in battle against mild snow
falling on the flip side of the pane.

She'll never know again what snow means
or sense the depth of ice in a city pond at dark;
never recognize her youngest child's winter birthday.
Here, she lives beyond weather, glides past
seasons, clocks and calendars, skates forever
in the blue ozone of destroyed memory.

Leaving it all behind, I head out
to county roads where night is falling
like a dark pillow over Minnesota
countryside. Nothing lies ahead now
but the loop and swirl of blowing snow
beneath my tires, fanned-out

Like thinning ringlets on an old woman's head,
like the white silk my mother's hair is
when combed out at last for sleep.

Mother's Day Card

My mother's mind has sweetly washed away
but we continue laughing, great giggles
of hysteria rocking through us as she sees
the young orderly walking Lizzie by
and elbows me: "Aren't they cute?
They're so *antique!*" And I roar with her,
helpless in this comic grief.

It's a good night, her hands almost at rest
from the usual agitated picking
at her skirt. She softens every minute,
chiding me just mildly for the baby
she's certain I've left in the bureau drawer.
Pure coquette, she rolls her eyes and sighs
and we collapse in gales again.

Minutes later, changeable as air,
she'll shower me with garbled curses,
weeping with frustration for the word
she cannot find, and it's the same sorry mess
I'd forgotten for a moment,
some crazed imposter masquerading as her mind.

Mother of this gorgeous manic mirth,
tonight we're closer in our giddiness
than we've ever been in forty years.
I straighten out your lap robe carefully
and pick off small nubs of lint,
my mind already walking forward
to the hour when sleep will call my name

And I'll wrestle again the angel of failure,
exhausted with awareness
of every unwalked bridge of history
we never crossed, each lost possibility
you and I have known.

When

My mother with bright words falling from her mouth
again, my mother with dementia lifted
from her shoulders and the iron shawl of Alzheimer's
rusted into dust, my mother singing
her life back, dancing that silly waltz
in the kitchen with my brother Kevin's friend,
my mother standing in the ordinary light
doing ordinary things like ironing or making tea,
my mother *not* screaming garbled words
in the night, *not* afraid of things her brain
was losing, *not* fierce with rage, my mother
not wearing the shame of a diaper
or a curl of milky spittle on her chin,
not giving the bright wrong answer
to the question, my mother reciting
"I Never Saw A Moor" or "Where Go the Boats"
after bathtime with that long Boston "a"
of dahling, then yelling in the morning
you kids better hurry up or you'll be late,
my mother believing me when I told her smoke
on my clothes came from other girls' cigarettes,
my mother walking backward from the nursing home,
from the psych ward for the elderly at that hospital,
backward from the afternoon my father cried
when she ran into the kitchen cracking eggs
on the floor one by one, my mother
whom my friends said was more beautiful
than their own mothers, rustling
into the blue silky dress before the Princess Grace dinner,
my mother gardening under the usual summer sun, the sky
just as it was then, serene, unbroken.

Washing My Mother's Hair

Hours after
her breathing had grown softer
    shallow   and more occasional
until none of us could tell
the exact moment that it stopped,

    While her forehead
was still almost warm when I brushed
my cheeks against the peony-thinness
of her skin,   before
the austerity   of death

    Had filled
the hospital room
where we had sung to her
our childhood songs that morning
as she began to leave us,

    Fergus and I
washed our mother's hair
for the last time. Partly ritual
and partly practical, that desire
to anoint, touch, clean, make new

    And beautiful.
My brother warmed the water
in a metal basin and the nurse
brought shampoo. Someone found
a comb and I lifted her head

    In my arms
with my left elbow cradling her neck,
the way I'd held my own children
as infants, the same gesture
she must have used so many hundreds

Of times
with the nine of us until her body
knew that movement like a second
language, effortless as breath. The wave
in her thick white hair wilted

                As water
flattened it across her scalp.
We squeezed shampoo in
and began massaging, lathering,
our hands rubbing every strand before

                The final rinse.
Fergus towelled the limp curls
in circles and Grania combed them
out as the warm air of the hair-blower
rushed through us all.

                How lovely
she looked after we'd finished, how
fragrant her hair, how I almost believed
for an instant such an ordinary act
could bring her back.

The Poverty of Secrets

Gift, Unbidden

I've been sailing for centuries on a boat
of my own making, circling the world
toward something I could never name.
On the cliffs above I've seen the dancers
pirouetting, their bodies frame-frozen
like the death-chain at the end of Bergman's
Seventh Seal, and these are the moments
when I've thrown the boom, hurrying away
from the awful beauty of your face, the awful destiny
of having known you since before birth,
the pity of knowing just how gently
you must close that knowledge to me now,
and all my helpless want following you
the way a moth would crash and bump
against a light it craved, wanting only succor.

And if I should stop here beyond these few days
of happenstance but then step back on board,
if I should never tell you how your tenderness
had broken me so utterly, all the planets
would keep spinning in their proper orbits
and the world would hum on, but some gift of gold
you offered with no debt attached
would become sacrilege.

I didn't know, I didn't know
your name before. When I leave this calmness
of the Sound for the open sea again
I want my wake to float back your way
this bundle of small offerings:
three deep-red poppies I climbed the hill
to pick for you; one perfect sheet
of blue hand-blown glass I'll always see your soul as;
an oar, in case you're ever islanded again,
and every charged atom of gratitude
I own.

Walking The Distance

All last night I paced the beach
through sightless fog. The air was dense
as gauze, a deeper whiteness than
I've ever known, and only faith
allowed belief that sand lay
beneath with each blind step I took.

I was headed back, love,
trailing the bag of my raggedy doubts,
carrying the child no larger than a whisper
under the skin beneath my sweater,
the roar of ocean all around me
and your voice in the distance
calling us both beloved, a magnet of light

Pulling the single pole of us
across two thousand miles
back home, back home to you.

Elegy For The Lost Ones

Fíona and Michael have gone. Gone to the lake
of lost children, gone to the woods
of dead possibility, gone to meet their small
friends. They are not orphans, for
their parents never claimed them, never
owned them. No mother ever felt
that rapid heartbeat or the nudge of fist
against her belly; no father ever walked
the cries of one to sleep, whispering "mine"
over and over into a newborn's cheek.

Under the surface of the lake where light
never reaches they swim forever, all
the children of never-land. I see them
wraith-like and naked, wrapping coils of loose
green seaweed around their bodies like blankets.
I see them in the forest lacing twigs
above their heads, building and rebuilding
a difficult, intricate pattern of shelter,
some other dwelling to call home.

Dream, Late Pregnancy

"I've found the tree from which I'll cut the wood
to build a cradle for our child," he said.

My mouth filled with sawdust and I couldn't
answer, wishing it were so,
the fetus kicking up a storm inside my belly
as I bent to straighten files
of prospective parents eager to adopt
the child his father wanted to relinquish,
and bent again in pain at the cruelty
of the dream.

Christ! What I would have given
to see him sawing wood like that,
gold chips of white oak raining
down upon his arms as he shaped
and smoothed the rough edges
of the baby's cradle,
a loving, honest man bonded
to his unborn son.

The Other Woman, Revisited

So now he's back again and you become
the same fool you were once before
but doubly so, with all the benefits
of insight that a decade should accrue.
Funny how the landscape hasn't altered,
the woods of self-deceit still green
and winsome with their pretty paths leading
nowhere, and all the trees bent with promises,
their disappointing fruit unripened yet.
But it's sweeter in the forest
on that bed of leaves where he makes love
to you on lunch hours, easier
somehow to stay than to leave
for that other world where you must trail
him ten feet back in a crowd, worrying
about the fresh smudge of earth on his suitcoat
that his wife or someone in the office
might detect, and trying to balance that
against the child thickening in your belly
whose faint, bewildered cries will one day grow
to howls for the father whom he'll never know.

Hospital

When memory is absent, where does one
begin? A whole range of days lost
to the pleasant executioner
in light green scrubs, that giver
of the cool anesthesia
before the storm of electricity
strips the pinnings of the mind away –

When the needle pierced her arm
she fought unconsciousness like a dog,
struggling to recall what had ever
made her give herself away like this.
It didn't matter, afterward.
She lacked remembrance of any deep thing
she'd done or thought for weeks, years.

They soothed her wound with promises,
the fierce headache with Tylenol,
wheeling her back to her room
confused, in her recovery, about
what harm had been done to whom.
She had a month to wonder how it was
to heal this way, obliterating segments
of the past one can't digest
with blue voltage to the brain.

She remembers several little things
from last summer – the old Ford
going under, the neglected garden
wilting in July. But not her middle
child's fifth birthday, or the courtroom
where she handed up her newborn
in a daze. It was all dream-like,
still, too difficult to track.
Her mind hurts, thinking of it.

One night, staring at the blurred air
from her sixth-floor window, she realizes
where she is, on the locked B-ward
at St. Joseph's Hospital.
And that's the moment she begins
the task of memory, calling up
every devil of depression she can name,
searching each hideout
of those deep black caves.

Tomorrow, she decides, she'll pretend
to swallow the regimented medicine,
disposing later of unwanted Lithium.
And then she will embark upon the work
of mending ravelled memory, patching it
together piece by piece, until she reaches
the first stitch she began –

A survivor, after all, who someday will emerge
with the multi-colored quilt of memory,
that old familiar blanket under which she slept
before this forced reign of amnesia
claimed her mind.

Through The Looking Glass

Castlehaven Cabins, Lake Superior

The window over the lake was streaked with rain,
a violent sideways slash of wetness
gusting upward. But I could see Superior
well enough to want to lose myself
in its great embrace; could see you, too,
writing steadily in your left-handed stance
at the cabin table.
White caps raised the waves beyond the shore
to beaten peaks and the great lake
frothed and turned, a huge, relentless motion
echoing back upon itself.

Something happened as I sat. I can't say what,
exactly, but some willing crack inside my mind
opened to the grey force outside me
and I slipped right through it
to the world between two worlds, that country
just beyond the looking glass.
It was the future that I saw, love,
and you weren't in it, anywhere.
The boys and I were older, walking down a summer road
alone, and we wore that raw look of peace
survivors wear as they leave the burning house
without scars. We held hands tightly,
heading home.

I watched us travelling without you
and felt such sadness for what might have been
that I nearly turned and told you what I'd seen.
I watched myself watching all of this
and knew with helpless certainty
I couldn't stop what hadn't yet occurred.

I watched the rain bead to bubble on the glass
and burst, watched Superior blacken
into sudden night and finally felt
my legs asleep beneath me in the big chair.
Your notebook was black and fat with words
and your back was turned from me,
completely unaware of where I'd been.

The Window of Regret

We would always wish it to be otherwise.
That the four food groups lived in pleasant harmony
in our daily lives, our bodies pure
from working out; that we'd bagged the trash
the night before and hauled it down
before the garbage trucks arrived at dawn.
That we'd heeded hurricane warnings,
dropped the whole material past and left
with souls intact. Or spoken crucial words
to a friend before the plane roared away
and it was suddenly too late. That our parents
knew the full dimension of our love
while they were still most alive.
That one or both of us had shown more faith
and the twin stems our bodies were
had not conceived such rancor or mistrust.
That we could wake tomorrow
with the world's enormous sadness gone
and the garden cleansed to innocence; the apple
luminous and whole upon the branch,
never bitten.

Mother's Day

This isn't the day to phone me, absent father
of the child I carried all last year.
For once your silence is a blessing,
for if I'd told you that I planted flowers
in the hot May sun for each of the boys
for hours today, you'd be uncomfortable,
afraid to name or ask about the missing one
you'd just as soon forget was born.
He's walking, now, I hear; in June
he'll turn a year.

It's funny how I see each boy uniquely
in these bedding packs; how, for Naoise,
I sunk sunny marigolds; for Conor,
deep pink petunias, their somber velvet
weighty as that child's thought.
For Devin I bought something new,
a spiky white plant whose name I never learned,
thick-stalked and beautiful, with a bloom
like tear-petals poking out of stone.

The black earth soothed me as I dug,
remembering their very different births
and how I held them each as if the world
has just begun, dizzy with terror
at my love for them. We planted all afternoon,
the two boys and I, and I write to say
we named the white flower Brian,
packing mounds of sweet spring dirt
carefully around his new family's roots.

The Poverty of Secrets

While Cupid slept, Psyche cleaned her knife
until it shimmered with intent, the metal
lingering on her wrist as she checked
its sting, felt the coolness of its bite.
It was almost sharper than her pain.
For one year now, she had loved him quietly
in darkness; had borne a son to him, abandoned
to the razored mountaintop the way
she'd been herself that night, when he slipped
the hooded cloak upon her neck and beckoned
her to follow. Now her need was knowledge,
not revenge: what beast lay in his face
that she could never see? What god forbade
one look between them, making love?

At midnight Psyche lit the small brass lamp
and watched the oil sputter as it grew
to orange flame. Cupid stirred and sighed
as Psyche turned to him, all her rage
and longing etched upon her face. When
she learned she loved him in that broken light,
when she felt the blade of grief carving
small impossibilities across her ribs,
those same ribs her unborn son once nudged,
her hands began to tremble and she spilled
the hot lamp oil onto his arm.

Thrust from sleep to terror, Cupid fled
and wandered thorny mountains in a daze
that drifted into weeks, to years, as every place
he searched, Psyche's face appeared
to him among the bushes bent with roses,
a face struck equally with radiance as with doubt,
arms lifting high the heavy knife
above her in the lamplight, calling,
out his name.

Of Boys And Men

The General Boasts

The Persian Gulf War, January, 1991

His men can survive on this:
one dog, a rabbit and a pair of rats.
We'll do, he says, anything
it takes.

A fine powder of sand
grits the bony innards
of this smallest of mammals.
Chewing, one man vomits quietly.

Who am I, he wonders,
to rip the flesh
off my brother's rabbit,
playmate of my own children's rabbits?

And who are they, he asks,
here to bargain to the death
over oil? He sizes up his next test,
the general's scrawny, whimpering dog.

Across the desert, sleek stealth bombers
sinew through the blackened sky
as poison gas drifts upward
like a summer blizzard.

A young reservist dreams she hears
the ancient drumbeats begin.
Beneath her fingers lies the cold steel
of her weaponry; in her heart, the certainty

She's taken part
in the clear moral end
of this planet.

One dog, a rabbit, and a pair of rats.

When The Bough Breaks

Three boys perch
on an orange dumpster
behind Red's Supermarket,

black silhouettes
caps askew, legs angled
in easy adolescent grace,

the thick night-glitter
of Franklin Avenue
below them like a feast.

They'll still be sleeping,
maybe dreaming
of that new girl down the block

when the sun shocks awake
the first gentle drunks
lying curbside on the avenue,

and the newest batch of condoms
by the porno theatre
curls in sweet summer heat.

Those boys – those boys.
How we love and mourn them,
skittering clouds before storm.

The Treasure Box

for Conor

In it, he puts assorted ikons from a child's day:
one Batman cape sans the absent hero;
the feather I brought him from Puget Sound, grey-
ruffled from the suitcase ride two weeks ago;
a sprinkling of Schilling's cake decorations thrown
in like ruby dust, glittering red glass
in the felt-bottomed box he made, his own.
This child who's most worried me, whose only trespass
was uncertainty about which parent might leave
him first or love him least, now amazes me
with a plain painted case, and I believe
him capable of magic; anything. I see
him for the boy I never knew, in silence
constructing gentle power from the violence.

The Children Beckon Late

Dense with sleep
and thick with midnight hibernation,
they lumber to my bed at 4:00 a.m.

Little bear cubs, winter's almost thawed.
I can shelter you from nightmare,
wrap you in the starry folds

Of my blue mother-quilt,
but only for a time.
When adulthood summons,

You'll forget the hundred backrubs
that soothed a child's deep panic,
and that will be all right.

Other women will hold you, measure
the grown male fears of you,
and gently draw you from the cave

To springtime's light.
I wish these women grace and courage
now, as I meet another sleepless night.

Under It All

The locked beauty of my sons in sleep:
they swim transparent there, unburdened
by the weight of gender and its deep
divides, that mass of land they can't transcend.
The last words they used on me tonight
was their supreme insult: "You're a girl,
Mom, and that's it." Called to fight,
I fought the urge to strangle or to whirl
them senseless on the bed and stopped
before the ninja-turtle instinct summoned reason
clean away. Then Naoise yawned and swore
he wanted just one kiss. I thought of men
and boys, and wept. I thought of all of this,
and mourned my dolphins' hidden gentleness.

All Is Calm, All Is Bright

for Naoise, Conor and Brian

Praise the tree, the cranberry-popcorn garlands
strung after dinners in December,
my small boy-terrorists' conversion
to positive reflection. Sing its "ancient"
preschool ornaments, each happy yelp
of recognition by those boys. Let our new
guinea pig, Spooky, roam freely on the floor
among pine needles, and "Radio Ahhs" play
"O Christmas Tree" once more. That star
that Naoise climbed the couch and windowsill
to crown the tree with – let it bless our house
with faith and reverence for birthdays
bigger than Santa Claus. And when
the world's armaments grow silent
for their annual truce, when all the lights
are out except the white bulbs circling
the midnight crèche, let me stop to celebrate
those boys in anxious sleep upstairs and send
a silent wish to that other child I love,
sleeping in St. Paul. As grace abounds tonight
and magic hums its low background song,
I'll climb the stairs in grateful prayer
for every spark of love that lives.

Long Distance

Time rushes backward through the wires —
their voices on the phone tonight small
as early childhood, reeling me back
to Naoise with peas stuck in his ears, to Conor
in that store hissing to the kind clerk
that God *gave* him that truck,
so bug off. Hanging up, I thought of the kid
this morning doing handstands
on the lawn, how I wanted to grab the bright coin
of him and squander its riches all on me
until love and poverty were the only things left.

We always want what's leaving us:
our sons like meteors, speeding away
from us toward adolescence;
that moment in October when light
charges leaves and limbs equally
and then vanishes; the song
whose words slip away in sleep,
troubling our morning coffee.

Talk to me, babies, rub the ocean's joy
into the mouthpiece until I feel the salt
on your lips as you answer me
in monosyllables, *nope*, *yep*, *'Kay*, *bye*,
holding back the thing
you don't know how to give.

Mother / Son

His room is adolescent male, his own
retreat against the gust of female light
his mother casts around him. He can't remember
that she knew him first as body
of her own body, swimming dark
inside her like a fish, first son.

Years she marveled at his flesh, this son.
There were no boundaries to divide his own
skin from hers; even in the dark
night of nursing they were one light
rocking by the window, one body.
This sense of peace is something she remembers.

He tires of her repetitions: *remember
your homework, remember the trash.* What son
wouldn't? The way she hovers over, a body
couldn't breathe. He'd die to make his own
life far away from her, to light
the house on fire and run into the dark

where no one knew him as a child, the dark
house in flames, a dream he can't remember.
He studies his legs in the bath, the curls of light
hair sprouting reward for any son
along with height and Adam's apple, his own
fierce trophies, these changes of the body.

She loves his colt-like awkwardness, his body
lurching upward overnight from dark;
the way the Dodgers baseball cap he owns
is angled backward. She remembers
him minutes old; how foreign now, this son
who hides from her and turns away from light.

Headphones on, he turns off the light.
The bed's a little short for his body.
He gathers what he knows as firstborn son
around him, unravels into dark
and sleep, trying hard to remember
what part of him is hers and what's his own.

She surrenders him, her son, the dark
night's body shielding what each owns.
Years from now, they'll each remember light.

Deora Dé

for my father

We walked through a tunnel of fuschia
and he called the bushes *Deora Dé*.
"From the Irish," he said, *Tears of God*.
How like him it was to pull his other language
from the air like that,

Threading the red blaze of color
and its teardrop song to the sorrow spent
by one creating it, petal by detailed petal
added to a burden of immense particulars
in a world still daily being made.

My father – his thin shoulders angling
through the patched tweed jacket,
our hands linked by the old stories,
fused history cast in common bone.
And the wild fuschia light
on the West Cork mountains
that October afternoon.

In The Name Of The Children
Waco, Texas, April 1993

In the name of the children we stormed their bunkers,
gas bursting from our canisters
like excited snakes.
It all happened so damn fast.
Flames peeled the roof off without thought,
and in seconds the black walls blew out.
It was so hot, wet April sod
sizzled to the touch.

When it was over, when smoked choked the air
before the fire trucks arrived and noted it
impossible that anyone survived,
I saw a charred grey arm jerking
on the ground, attached to a child
whose mind was still intact.
She could have been mine, or anyone's.

That night every network tuned us in
as we shoveled our overkill into sterile bags
and picked through stench-filled rubble
for the rest. One by one,
America's other children slept
while we sweated and puked and wept
till dawn, when the new shift began.

I left then, to see my daughter off to school,
glancing only once at the cirrus-clouded sky.
But I thought I saw their faces there
above the ashes of the Branch compound,
their eyes with the too-bright look of panic,
and not one of them waving goodbye.

.

The One Who Swears
You Can't Start Over

Too Soon

John Engman, 1949-1996

The first and last time
I held your hands in mine
they radiated heat
beneath the IV's and other tubes.
I watched your chest rise and fall
with the forced breath
that respirators pump through lungs
and spoke to you of unsaid things
too long unsaid.

You looked at peace,
the deep sleep of the dreamer
swimming his coma out. Maybe
you were working on that new poem
with the marginal part
of your brain that remained,
maybe you were tipping back
an exquisitely chilled ale
in the noon heat of a June day,

Maybe inside that silent body
cells were furiously letting go
47 years of the world's imprints —
a sorrow here, a kiss there,
the small triumphs won. And
maybe you heard every voice
in the room, every past soul
you'd ever made laugh
telling you they'd miss you, John.

Grief

The way it comes from nowhere,
lapping at the half-healed heart
like a dog hoping to be loved
if he just keeps coming by to play.
Then later like a needle,
a high thin pain, the body
twisted double with it,
utterly undone.

Suddenly at a traffic light
someone walks exactly
as your mother walked,
that stoop, the slow look left
and right, the long coat
swishing below knees. Frozen,
your mind won't let your foot
release the clutch, and you're reeled
in again. Grief.

How long a memory lasts depends
upon so many things: the ruby shade
a rose can glow in August
and how it hooks you back
to her garden; whether or not
one of the boys had a fever
that Sunday morning when you
took the call; how much
alcohol or solitude can do; how little,
in the end. But grief, that thief,
softened by time or abandoned
with intent, doesn't budge; it is the one
constant that outlasts them all.

Six Years On

for Steve Arhelgar

(after James Dickey)

And now the green household is dark.
Night floats down gently,
a frond of shadow-ferns covering the roof.
Sleepers step into the netherland of dreams
and fish begin to surface from the glassy lake,
their flat bodies skimming water idly.
This is the moment the whole day
has been leaning toward, pushing
against pillars of light
until the hours toppled into dimness
like the slow fall of weightless bowling pins,
soundless, down.

Why is it darkness frees the dead?
Like laughter from the trail ahead
I know you're out there somewhere, wandering
but real as rain-blackened maple trunks
against cherry-orange leaves.
Six years now you're gone
and I can't recall one time
I could conjure up your face in daylight.
Tonight your eyes flare alive sure as stars
and I hear your reckless stride wearing down
the stairs. Who gave you right to walk these halls,
just because the green household is dark?

The wind through the poplars,
a low roar. A moon slides out
behind grey clouds, then disappears.
At this moment when I find myself

so unbearably rooted to this earth,
I wonder whether, when the bullet you sent reeling
through your brain found its mark,
you saw light or you saw dark. And I wonder, too,
if I held the power to hand you back your life again,
you'd accept it, now that the green household
is finally and forever dark.

Addressing The Voice That Says I Can't

Like learning to walk again,
the first awkward stumble of shoes –
but harder now, since once you did it well.
This conscious movement is a gritty effort,
pride and dust weighed in equal measure.

Talk to that voice, the one who swears
you can't start over. Do not soothe it
with silence; it is a swarm of dormant vipers,
years of whispered lies hissing in the brain.
And will not go away until addressed.

A small girl's utterance: *Daddy, I can't.*
Not good enough, not smart enough,
not brave enough to cross the bridge alone.
Not enough. And so the voice travels
to adulthood, until risk becomes a frozen thing
reduced to mute inertia.

Listen: culture has teeth, has guard dogs,
big batons. Cross the bridge, my darling,
you are the woman it has weathered storms
for, refusing to rot. See, the greying planks
hold their old shape, yet.

Pet their dogs, tame those stiff hairs soft
with your touch. Perfect your twirl,
if necessary. Or bite back. But put your shoes
on. Learn and do. Keep on going, one foot
leading the next. You can, you can, you can.

Ordinary Contentment

"What hurt me so terribly all my life until this moment?"

In June the two-inch cosmos flowers
grow to willowy stalks and bloom
their pink pinwheel hearts out.
Such shock the ordinary logic
of growth brings, love springing
from the earth without effort.

Tonight the kettle gleams a dull yellow
under the stove-lamp and the swing creaks
gently on the porch. Neighbors breathe
in unison, each house webbed in sleep.
At this moment all storms at bay
and the never-far-away black caves

at my shoulder lose their terror,
leaking light like bright forgiveness
from their tight pores. This is the hour
every drama's facet wears down
to the plain nugget of the common thing:
the purr of cat humming

While a foot rubs its back,
the sheen of moisture on my daughter's cheek
when I touch her baby skin
in the evening heat, the blessing of rain
falling, falling on the purple mountains
of New Hampshire; and this sudden wild gratitude

for the daily here, the now.

both poem title and epigraph taken from Jane Kenyon's "Wood Thrush"

Abandoned Poems

I think of them as orphans,
the birth certificate unsigned, no
one willing to own up to them.

Branded unachievable,
that constant knowledge
is their load,

The labels straight pins to the bone:
*"half-formed promises," "contrived
endings," "confused voice throughout."*

I see rows of them, slump-shouldered,
line up at night, seek shelter
as they jostle ink to inky backs,

Never knowing how
their parents worked on them, shaping
and drafting and shaping, loving

Their flaws even as they sliced
their darlings into amputees, even
as they roughed them up

With one furious version
after the next, until what they believed
themselves to be originally

Split into shards,
pieces of bone teacup
thrown against the wall,

The writer seized by loathing.
What sadness, at the end
of day, turning one's back

On the unready colt
wandering out the stable door
on legs too new to hold him.

Dinner At The Frost Place

for Susan Roney O'Brien

Brazilian music and the slow sax
of Stan Getz steaming in the kitchen
to the pulse of simmering garlic.
Sweet zucchini sheds its speckled skin
in Susan's sauce and Elizabeth sambas slowly
across the floor, five men in a trance
behind her. We have cast a spell on anyone
who enters here tonight, three women
armed with poetry and the charm of food.
Our arugula lies succulent and tender
around the bed of wet cucumbers
and red tomatoes, our eggplant swells
with mozzarella in the oven, our sauce
gains velocity as it heats. We sway
to this summer music with loose hips
and sweaty cheeks, our cooking spoons
raised like wands. Such ripeness!
And now the wine, a gentle red fire
in the stomach....... Come moonlight,
bread nearly flies from the oven
and "The Girl From Ipanema" throws away
her combs. None of us has ever known
such lyric food, such bardic guests,
such high July happiness before.

Chamomile

This morning walking the usual trail
I noticed chamomile, its pale root
tapered as a mousetail entering the dirt,
the green nub of its flower spiked
with a halo of yellow hairs, a furry aureole.
Crushing the warm bulb between my thumb
and finger I inhaled the future scent
of steeping tea from mashed, dried greens.
And I thought of its power to soothe
the nightmares from a child's brow,
to slow the racing heart of the man on death row,
to calm the earth's tilt, even for just
a millisecond. I almost missed it,
common weed among the scrubgrass –
the sheer tenacity it owns
in springing back when walked on, the secrets
packed in the heart of its densely woven bud.

In Time

Everything reveals itself in time.
I simply counsel patience when I feel
your soul alive like this so close to mine.

Inside its shell the oyster sleeps in brine,
its hidden pearl glowing and surreal.
Everything reveals itself in time.

In April tulip hearts begin their climb
from earth to light; the world starts to heal.
Your soul's alive like this so close to mine.

We work to unlock mysteries and find
our palms raw and empty, so we kneel.
Everything reveals itself in time.

Come evening, stars tumble, then align
themselves in constellation. Can they anneal
your soul, alive like this, so close to mine?

Much effort makes the perfect rhyme
and waiting has its worth, its own appeal.
Everything reveals itself in time,
your soul alive like this so close to mine.

Driving The Coast Road To Dingle

for John Sweetser 1919-1998

The light was thinning. Dusk fell
in soft haphazard clumps on the sheep,
the hills, the long streak of sea
below, the boys sprawled across
the back seat, their smell of wet wool,
of child-musk and sleep.

Ahead, two horse-trailers took the curves
slow and their brake lights deepened
on-off, on-off, a red glow. Who
could hear me singing on this road
above the sea, who could hear
the leaps and dives my heart made
on-off, on-off, as I drove?

We headed west into dark
toward the harbour-town
whose name repeated in my brain
like rain sweeping now
across the windshield. The Volvo
skimmed hedgerows to the left
and my hands gripped the steering wheel
a few times before the boys woke up.

At that moment
stars began to push
their white necks through
the shawled sky above.
I knew then there was no
inch of earth, no
other world than this
I loved.

The Lockmaker

I've designed each perfect numbered wheel
to turn upon mechanical command.
Gently I clean the residue of history,
dirt lodged between the slots of able cogs.

It's precision that I crave, any form
hewn without mistake. I loathe inaccuracy,
the sloppy anarchy of human hands
that bend and give and usually fail.

My locks adorn Manhattan's best, burnished
brass, dependable as Lloyd's of London.
The trust those blue-haired women place in me
allows me easy sleep, my tumblers custom-built to last.

They are so exquisitely exact, my best
beloved locks. Tonight I turn my key
and all that hard-won symmetry unravels
without warning, some failure of a minor untuned cog,

The past alive and reeling in the shuttered room,
gold patina stripped to tin: my mother's face,
Richard's eyes, the baby's small, helpless breath, all
the doors I've tried so hard to close behind me,

Ghosts pressing through a narrow keyhole
made for one specific, private turn,
the machinery of loss clicking into motion;
the ruin, dear God, of a lock undone.

Three Wishes For Brian

That
you know your belovedness
to each mother

Whom you own;
to the father who claimed you
as a falling star

Prized
among multitudes
of hot silver;

To your brothers
who have high-fived
the toddler-photo of you

Holding a fish
for years now   as they've passed it
on the refrigerator door.

Child
of my heart, how you've grown
into your long-stemmed body!

Four-and-a-half-years
tall, five years later, your
glad spirit

Bells, bends
each of our lives with music
I can at last and only

Call joy.

At This Moment

And if I have nothing to say
and all the words inside my brain
are hollowed out, scraped clean, gone,
then let nothingness stream forth
in rows of blazing zeroes.
Let emptiness be the still lake it is
where I coast in my small boat
fishing for the thing I cannot find,
the lake where stones travel
searching lifetimes for the bottom.
Let silence come like animals
in the dark mountain night,
watchful yet unafraid, licking my body
with tenderness the way a mother bear
licks her cubs, less to clean them
than to give them strength.
Let the absent words dissolve
before they're formed
and the fret and strain of pulling
one sentence toward the next
slacken, until all that's left
is something wild and musical,
one note without speech.

Homage To The Common

How I love the blazing dailiness
of this world, the way my shoes
wear down their heels in the same spot
each year; the gene-print of freckles
on my children's cheeks, the plain truth
that dust-balls breed, regardless;
the unmade beds and other signs
of absent domesticity, the late-night hum
of the furnace pumping out its heat,
even the knots in my shoulders
I've known since childhood.

I celebrate alike the lumpy August lawn
awash with acorns and the first new snow
which tempers any memory of wrong;
my aging Ford Escort and the slush
that city buses sling across its windshield,
the pageantry of light each morning
from the east, strong coffee
halved by cream; that in these last late years
of the 20th century, this planet
keeps on spinning toward some destiny
beyond our knowing. And always,

How utterly my friends astonish me
with their simple ordinary faith and care
for this or that. For the common grace
of all of it, the way the earth's
relentless lovely roots pull us deeper
in, I offer blessings, praise,
amazement.

Those We Carry With Us

Not the vendor selling hot roasted chestnuts,
sweet as the mashed white meat inside
the broken shell is. Not the man himself,
his Rastafarian braids electric as his smile.
Not the kindly mayor of our childhoods,
gaily tossing candy from the one-car float
of small-town Halloween.

        Even the dead, we lose,
eventually, pieces of them slipping from our arms
against our wills, like heavy trays we can
no longer hold. A glass breaks; we go on,
sewing the sharp pebble of loss safely into hems
or pockets. All our lives elaborate distractions
will fret for our attention, papers beckon,
sirens call our names. For all our ignorance
we know what's worth holding onto, can sense
whom we're bound to, if not why –

        My Polish friend
of the exquisite poems, the blue tattooed number
throbbing on her wrist as she held my hand
in both of hers somewhere in Los Angeles
while I cried; the travelling man I gave my soul
to at nineteen; the small angel of innocence
who guards me when the darkness comes;
the boys' shouts outside the kitchen window
and their faces later, deep in velvet sleep;
strangers, whose intimate connection
was made holy by a single glance;

These are the ones
who walk with us, bound lightly as the sheen
of cobweb lacing the hibiscus tree, bound tightly
over matter, distance, birth. In my dreams
I see them trailing in the shadows of the horses,
silent in the desert night. I finger the strands
which link them to my caravan and marvel
at such wealth. They are my crew, my absolutes.
I will carry them with me, always.